Animal Math

Taking Away with Tigers

Tracey Steffora

Heinemann
LIBRARY

Chicago, Illinois

Edited by Daniel Nunn, Abby Colich, and
Sian Smith
Designed by Joanna Hinton-Malivoire
Picture research by Elizabeth Alexander
Production by Victoria Fitzgerald
Originated by Capstone Global Library Ltd

**Library of Congress Cataloging-in-
Publication Data**
Steffora, Tracey.
Taking away with tigers / Tracey Steffora.
pages cm—(Animal Math)
Includes bibliographical references and index.
ISBN 978-1-4329-7563-0 (hb)
ISBN 978-1-4329-7570-8 (pb)
1. Subtraction—Juvenile literature. 2. Tiger—Ju-
venile literature. I. Title.

QA115.S7774 2014

513.2'12—dc23   2012049449

Acknowledgments
The author and publisher are grateful to the
following for permission to reproduce copyright
material: Shutterstock pp.4, 6, 8, 10, 11, 12, 14,
16, 17, 18 (© Eric Isselee), 5 (© Nick Biemans), 9
(© An Van de Wal), 17, 18 (© Iakov Filimonov),
20, 21 (© Volosina), 21 (© J. McPhail), 22 (©
Cynthia Kidwell).

Front and back cover photographs of a
white tiger reproduced with permission of
Shutterstock (© Iakov Filimonov). Front cover
photographs of Bengal tigers reproduced with
permission of Shutterstock (© Eric Isselée).

We would like to thank Elaine Bennett for her
invaluable help in the preparation of this book.

Every effort has been made to contact
copyright holders of any material reproduced
in this book. Any omissions will be rectified in
subsequent printings if notice is given to the
publisher.

Contents

Some words are shown in bold, **like this**. You can find them in a glossary on page 23.

Taking Away Tigers

Look! There are four tigers in the jungle.

One tiger leaves and climbs a tree.
How many are left?

We take away to find out how many
are left.

Start with four.

Take one away.

Four take away one is three.

There are three tigers left.

When we take away something, we are **subtracting**.

$$4 - 1 = 3$$

Counting Book

Here are the four tigers together again.

Now two tigers leave and go for a swim! How many are left?

Subtract to find out how many are left.

We can count back to find out how many are left.

Start with four. Count back two.

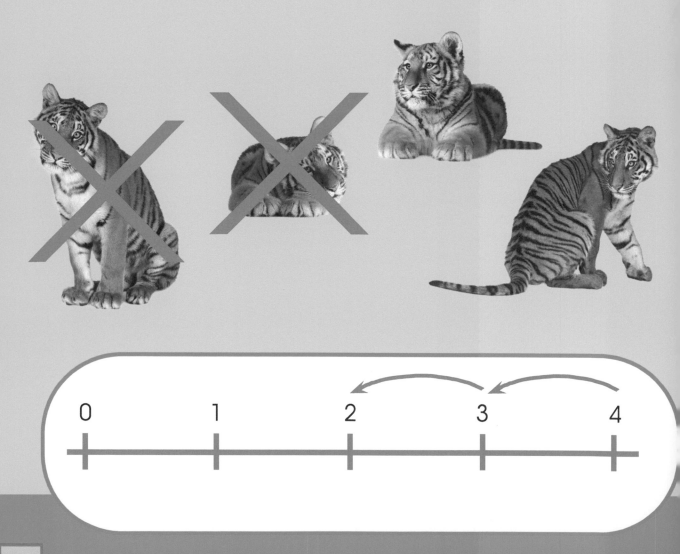

Four take away two **equals** two.

There are two tigers left.

$$4 - 2 = 2$$

Take Away All

All four tigers are back in the jungle.

They all run off to hide.
How many are left?

Start with four. **Subtract** four.

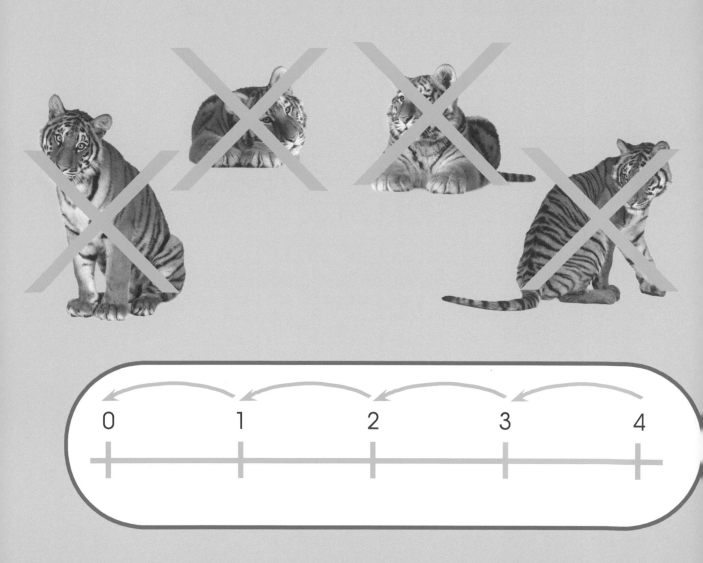

Four **minus** four is zero. Minus means something has been taken away. Zero means none or nothing.

There are no tigers left.

$$4 - 4 = 0$$

Comparing Groups

Let's look at two groups of tigers. There are four orange Siberian tigers in this group.

There are three white Bengal tigers in this group.

How many more orange Siberian tigers are there?

We **subtract** to find out how many more.

Compare both groups of tigers. Take away the smaller number from the bigger number. This will tell you how many more orange Siberian tigers there are.

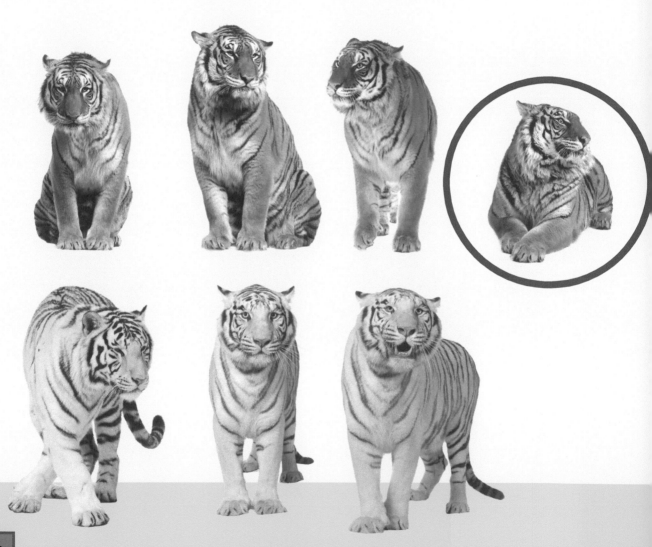

Four **minus** three is one. Minus is another way of saying take away.

There is one more orange Siberian tiger than white Bengal tiger.

How Many Are Left?

Tigers like to eat meat. Here are five steaks.

A tiger eats three of the steaks. How many steaks are left?

5 – 3 = ?

Answer on page 22.

Tiger Facts

- A group of tigers is called a streak.

- No two tigers have the same stripes.

- Tigers can leap up to about 30 feet!

- You can hear a tiger's roar from 2 miles away!

- Tiger **cubs** stay with their mother for two or three years before living on their own.

Answer
page 21: There are two steaks left.

Math Glossary

compare look at two or more things to see how they are the same and how they are different

equals = This sign says equals. You use it to show the answer.

minus – This sign says minus. You use it to take away one number from another number.

subtract another way to say take away, or minus

Tiger Glossary

cub the baby of a big cat, for example a young lion or a young tiger

Teaching Notes

Subtraction involves an understanding of quantity and being able to conceptualize *how many are left* after objects are *taken away*. Alternatively, it can involve the ability to compare two quantities to identify the *difference* between them. This title supports children's understanding of this operation through visual representation while introducing the mathematical vocabulary and symbols of subtraction.

Use this title to further support core operations and algebraic thinking standards:

- While reading the book aloud to the class, engage groups of children to play "tigers" and physically and visually act out the equations. Remember to reinforce language such as *take away*, *subtract*, *how many are left*, and *equal* when acting out each equation.

- Group children in pairs and give each pair a fixed quantity (10 or fewer) of similar objects (e.g., paper clips, counters, etc.). Have children take turns as they play a game in which one child puts all of the objects under one hand and then removes a quantity and displays it in a separate visible pile. The other child must then figure out how many are left under the hand ("You started with five. Then you took away two. There must be three left under your hand."). Have children record their answers using drawings, numbers and symbols, or word sentences.

Related Common Core Standards

CCSS.Math.Content.K.OA.A.1

CCSS.Math.Content.K.OA.A.2

CCSS.Math.Content.1.OA.A.1

CCSS.Math.Content.1.OA.B.3

CCSS.Math.Content.1.OA.C.5

CCSS.Math.Content.1.OA.C.6